Mysterious Patterns

Finding Fractals in Nature

Sarah C. Campbell

Photographs by
Sarah C. Campbell and
Richard P. Campbell

BOYDS MILLS PRESS
AN IMPRINT OF HIGHLIGHTS
Honesdale, Pennsylvania

For Graeme, Nathan, and Douglas

Acknowledgments: First, I want to thank the librarian who suggested I write about fractals. I am sorry I did not get your name. I learned most of what I know about fractals from Michael Frame, a mathematics professor at Yale University, who partnered with the late mathematician Benoit Mandelbrot to create the university's course on fractals. (I accessed the course online.) Michael generously agreed to share his expertise for this book. His contribution has been enormous, and I remain in awe and grateful. I had further help from Dr. Ewald Weibel, professor emeritus at the University of Bern, Switzerland. I appreciate Aliette Mandelbrot's willingness to share photographs. For the broccoli and much else, I thank Loy Moncrief and the other gardeners associated with the Jesse Gates Edible Forest at Wells Church.

Whenever anyone in my family writes a book, it becomes a family endeavor. I thank my husband, Richard; my parents, Dave and Patty Crosby; and my sisters, Emilye Crosby and Jessica Crosby-Pitchamootoo. I also thank my critical readers: Julie Owen, Carolyn Brown, Beth West, Jenny Mayher, and Peg Fisher. Finally, I would like to thank my fourth grade critique group at Davis Magnet IB School in Jackson, Mississippi: Brandon Allen, Jahari Bell, Amber Craft, Selase Dzathor, Gene Harrion III, Sydney Shaw, Mikayla Smith, Joseph Trigg, and Ashley Wells.

Text copyright © 2014 by Sarah C. Campbell
Photographs: Unless otherwise indicated here, photographs were taken by Sarah C. Campbell and Richard P. Campbell. 1: (inset) Bigstockphoto; 9: (icicles) Jenny Mayher; 18-19: iStockphoto; 20-21: NASA; 25: Ewald Weibel (creator of cast) and Barbara Kreiger (photographer); 22-23, 28-29: National Park Service; 32: photo of Benoit Mandelbrot courtesy of Aliette Mandelbrot, photo of radar cloaking device courtesy of Fractal Antenna Systems.

Boyds Mills Press
An Imprint of Highlights
815 Church Street
Honesdale, Pennsylvania 18431

Printed in Malaysia
ISBN: 978-1-62091-627-8
Library of Congress Control Number: 2013951286

First edition
The text of this book is set in Bell.

10 9 8 7 6 5 4 3 2 1

Glossary

Benoit Mandelbrot – [BEHN-wah Mahn-del-BROT]

cone – a solid shape with a circle for its base and a curved surface tapering evenly to a point

curve – a line having no straight part

cylinder – a solid shape with two parallel circular bases connecting with a curved surface

line – a long, thin mark that never ends

pattern – a design, with consistent characteristic form, of natural or constructed origin

sphere – a solid shape with a surface equally distant from the center at all points

surface – the outside or the outer covering of a thing

On a street, in a town, in a city,
familiar shapes are everywhere.

Some are spheres. Some are cones. Some are cylinders. These shapes were made by people.

For a very long time, people had names only for perfect shapes—
shapes with straight lines, smooth curves, or flat surfaces.

In a backyard, in a field, in a forest, things that grow in nature also have shapes. Some, like these tomatoes, are similar to but not exactly like those shapes.

Tomatoes are like spheres. Cucumbers are like cylinders. Icicles are like cones.

But many natural shapes do not look anything like the familiar, perfect shapes that people make. Instead of being straight, smooth, and flat, many natural shapes are rough, bristly, and bumpy. Most mathematicians and scientists thought natural shapes were too messy for people to categorize or to use to think about the world.

What shape is this?

Or this?

Or this?

Until 1975, we did not have a name for them.

Then a mathematician named Benoit Mandelbrot noticed similar patterns in these natural shapes. He agreed that the natural shapes, which he named "fractals," were different from perfect shapes, and didn't look much like one another. But he saw what they had in common.

Every fractal shape has smaller parts that look like the whole shape. Fractals are everywhere in nature, and can form in many different ways. A tree is a fractal. It starts with one shape that changes in the same way over, and over, and over again.

This tree starts with a stem, which splits into two branches, which each split into more branches, until the smallest branches split into twigs.

Many smaller parts of the tree—large branches with smaller branches and twigs—look like the whole tree, with its trunk and branches and smaller branches.

This head of broccoli is also a fractal. When broccoli is pulled or cut apart, each smaller part looks like the whole shape.

All fractals have parts that repeat at different sizes.

Queen Anne's lace grows flower heads with a fractal pattern, but they don't form like the tree. Instead of adding parts over and over and over again, the Queen Anne's lace produces a bud that opens over the course of days to reveal a fractal flower.

The large flower head is made of smaller flower heads, each on its own stem. The smaller heads, too, are made of even smaller five-petal flowers.

Fractals have edges that are jagged, wriggly, or craggy. This lightning splits off into many smaller-sized spikes in a jagged pattern. The pattern looks like the branches of a tree, though lightning forms in an instant. A tree takes years.

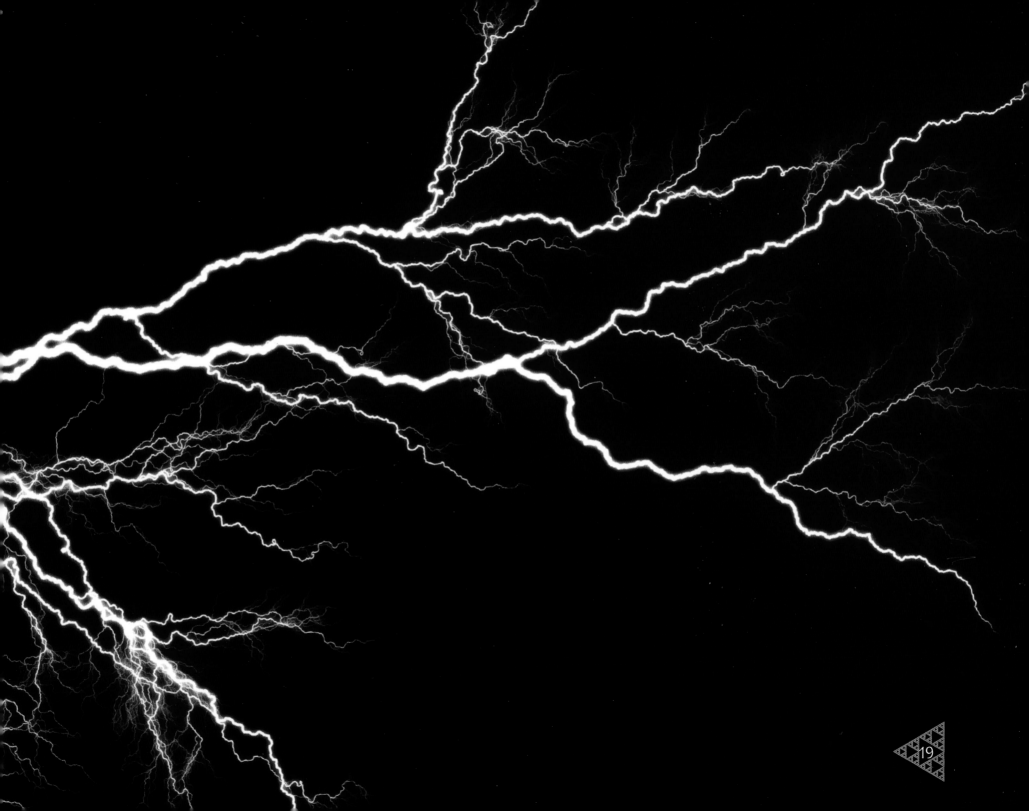

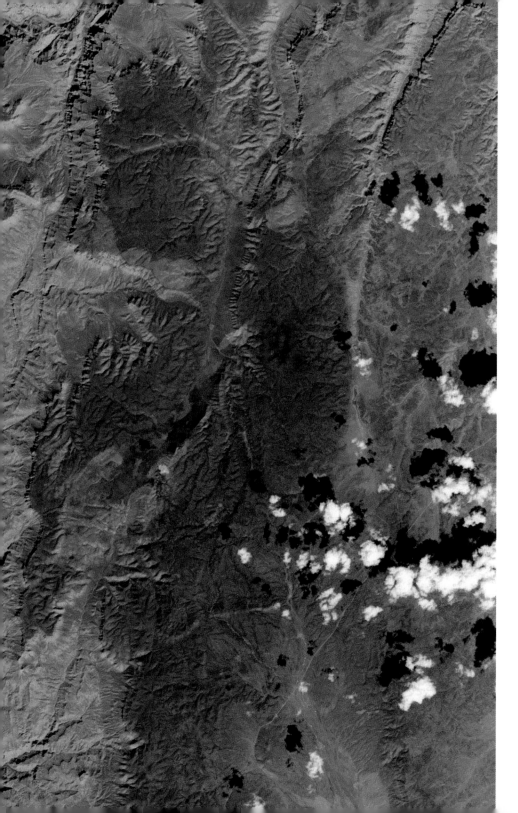

There are also fractal patterns on the earth's surface. Looking at the Colorado River from outer space shows us the fractal pattern of smaller rivers and streams that feed into one large river.

With fractals, the shape can change the same way over and over again by adding on, as when a tree grows branches, twigs, and leaves. Or, the shape can change the same way over and over again by creating new paths, as when water runs downhill and carves new channels in soil, rocks, and sand to create a river.

The Grand Teton mountain range formed at least nine million years ago when pressure below the earth's crust pushed one giant slice of rock against another so forcefully that it created towering peaks. Just like a head of broccoli is made of many smaller-sized florets, the Grand Teton mountain range is made of many smaller-sized mountains.

Some fractals form in a flash, like lightning, or in a growing season, like broccoli or Queen Anne's lace. Others, like trees or rivers or mountains, take hundreds or thousands of years.

There are also fractals inside of living things. This leaf's veins, which move water and plant food around, make a fractal pattern.

There are even fractals inside our bodies. Human lungs hold fractal shapes, which can be seen in airways, veins, and arteries. In the photo below, the airways are in off-white while the veins and arteries are in blue and red. (The veins and arteries are not present on the left side to better show the airways.) Lungs continue to develop inside our bodies throughout childhood, growing like a tree to fill the space inside our chests.

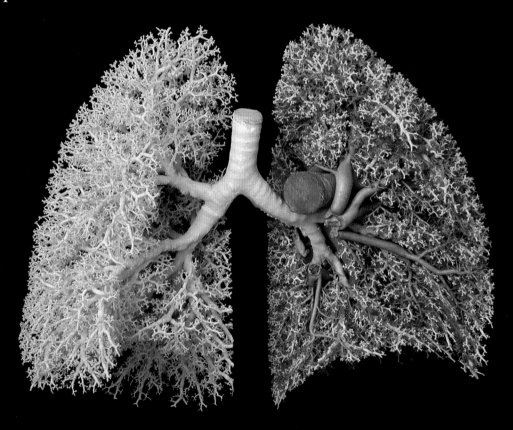

Not every pattern with similar shapes is a fractal. The sections on the outside of this pineapple form a repeating pattern, but each section is about the same size.

The skin markings on these swallowtail caterpillars also form a pattern, but instead of repeating at smaller sizes like broccoli or Queen Anne's lace, each stripe and dot is roughly the same size as all the others.

Because of what Mandelbrot discovered, and what he taught us about the patterns in our complex natural world, we can make sense of things that once seemed too messy, too small, or too large to understand.

Mandelbrot gave us a word—fractals—and an idea that helps us see the world in a whole new way.

The fractal shapes we see in trees, rivers, mountains, flowers, vegetables, and even in our own bodies, tell us a story about how things grow and change over time. The fractals may not be perfect or smooth, but they display patterns and an order of their own. Everywhere and every day, nature is forming fractals.

Make Your Own Fractal

This Sierpinski triangle is a fractal that does not grow in nature. It is called a geometric fractal.

Here are the steps for making one.

1. Draw a triangle with equal sides.
2. Draw a dot in the exact middle of each of the sides.
3. Connect the dots with straight lines. Now, your new shape breaks the original triangle into four smaller-sized triangles. (The one in the middle has a downward point.)
4. In each of the three triangles with an upward point, repeat steps 2 and 3.
5. You can keep repeating the steps, until no more smaller-sized triangles will fit.

The Sierpinski triangle is like the broccoli, Queen Anne's lace, and mountains. Each larger triangle splits into smaller triangles, and the pattern repeats.

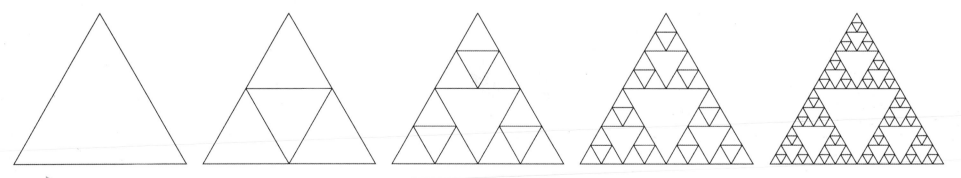

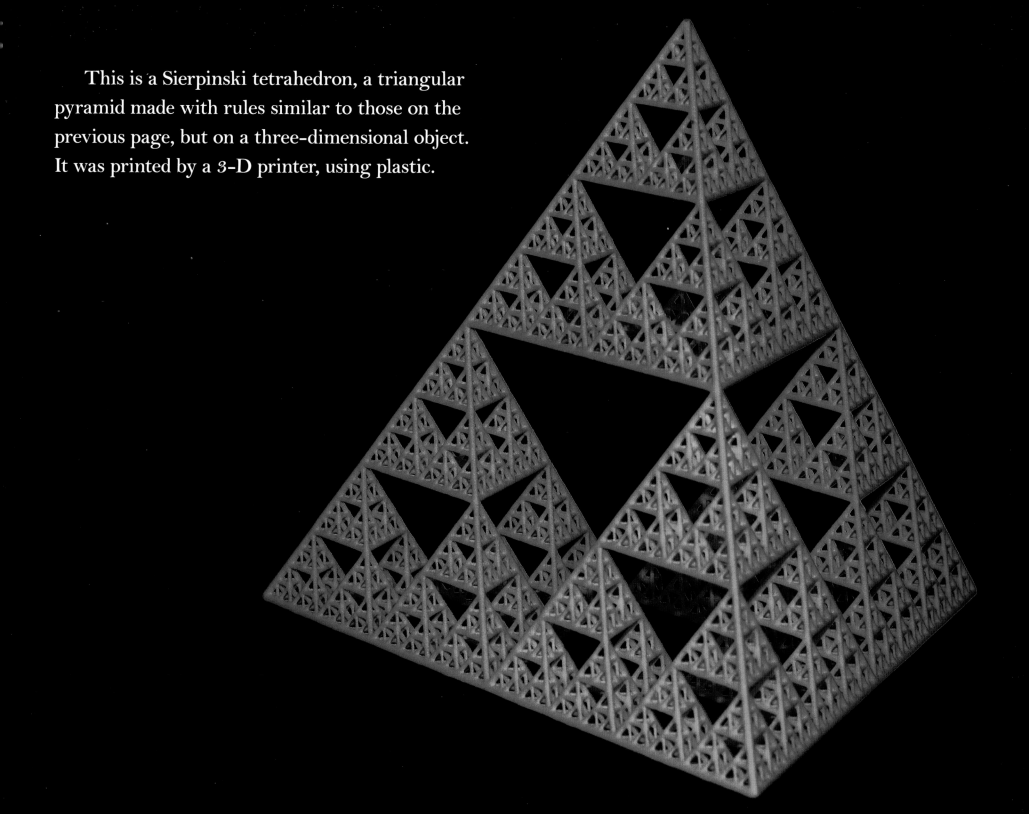

This is a Sierpinski tetrahedron, a triangular
pyramid made with rules similar to those on the
previous page, but on a three-dimensional object.
It was printed by a 3-D printer, using plastic.

The Boy Who Dreamed Up Fractals

This boy loved to look at maps, to read old geometry books, and to play chess. He worked as a toolmaker, and on a farm taking care of horses. In school he found that he didn't think the way other students and his teachers thought. He thought in shapes. And he loved finding connections between ideas. This boy was Benoit Mandelbrot.

When Benoit grew up and became a scientist, he studied odd things, things that didn't interest other scientists. He studied how often computers make mistakes when they talk with one another, how jagged coastlines are, how much it rains in different parts of a rainstorm. He studied how money moves on the stock market, and how galaxies are spread across the universe.

For many years, other scientists didn't pay any attention to him. But eventually Benoit saw an amazing connection. All the things he had been studying were related. They all were made up of little parts that looked like the whole thing. Benoit named these shapes fractals.

Nature works in clever ways. The mathematical rules that grow a frond of a fern also grow the whole fern. After Benoit showed scientists how to think about fractals, many saw that people can build things the same way nature does. The wiring of the Internet is fractal; so are cellphone antennas, devices to mix chemicals, fuel cells, new ways to store energy, even air conditioners—and this, a radar invisibility cloak. The rings are built of fractals. They bend radar waves around the center of the rings, making radar see around any object or person inside as if they weren't there.

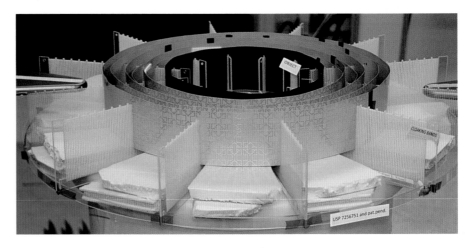

Nathan Cohen, who built this cloak, thinks the same idea can be applied to light, though the antennas would have to have much finer detail. Harry Potter's invisibility cloak would have been made of fractals.

You'll need to learn quite a bit more math to figure out how these things work, but it's very pretty math, and what wonderful worlds it will open for you.

Michael Frame teaches math at Yale University, where for twenty years he and Benoit Mandelbrot had great fun exploring the world of fractals together.